I0802213

I Do My Best!

Working Hard

Lela Lawson

SOCIAL AND EMOTIONAL LEARNING FOR THE REAL WORLD™

Rosen Classroom™

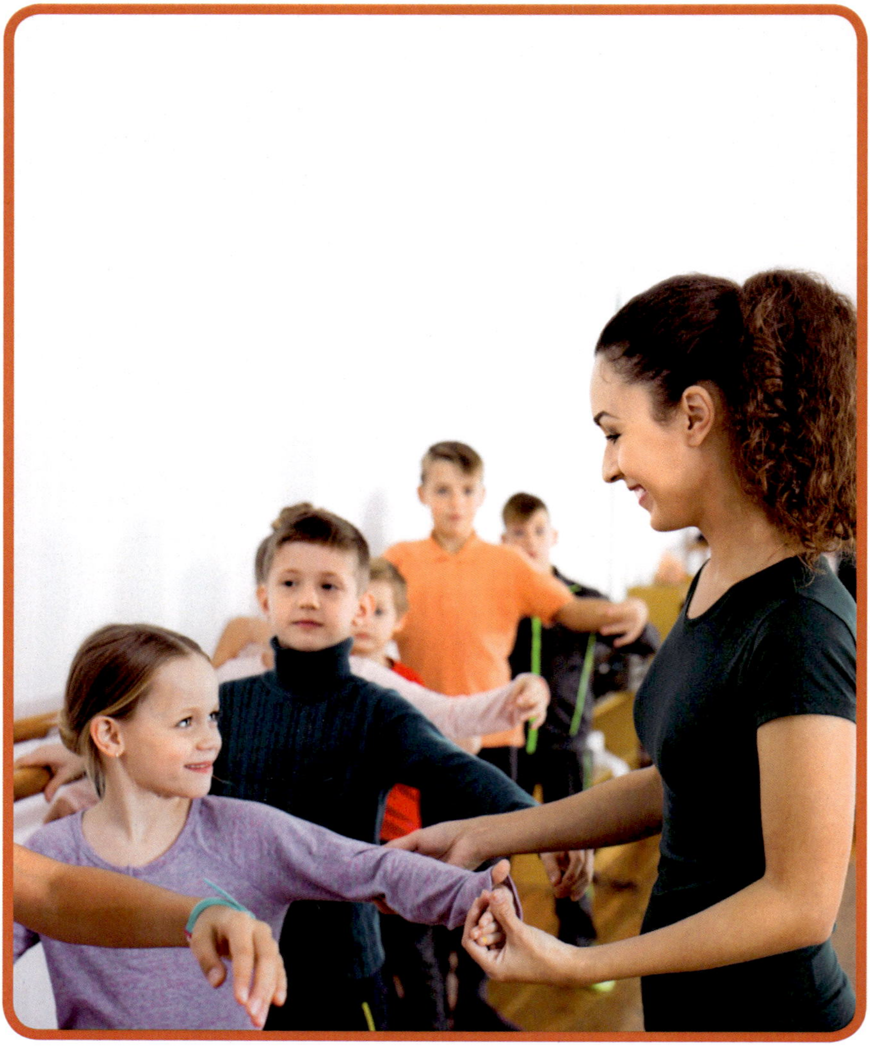

I can do it.

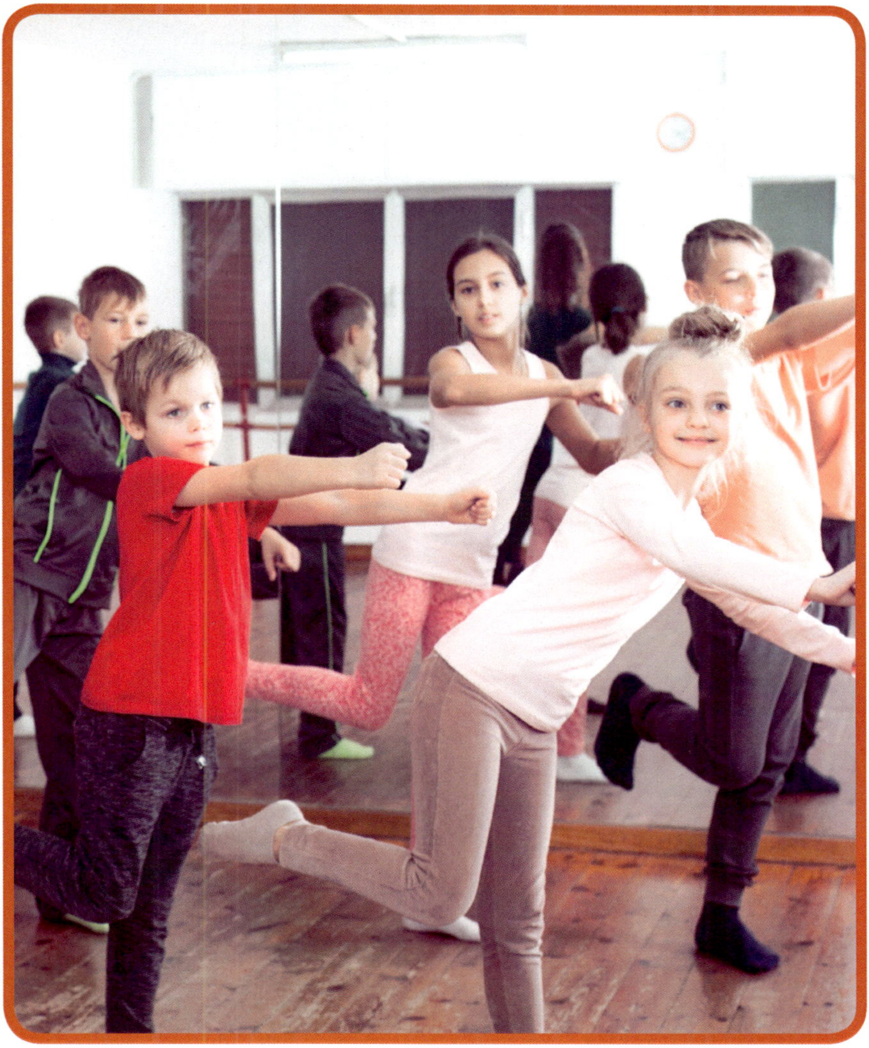

I can kick.

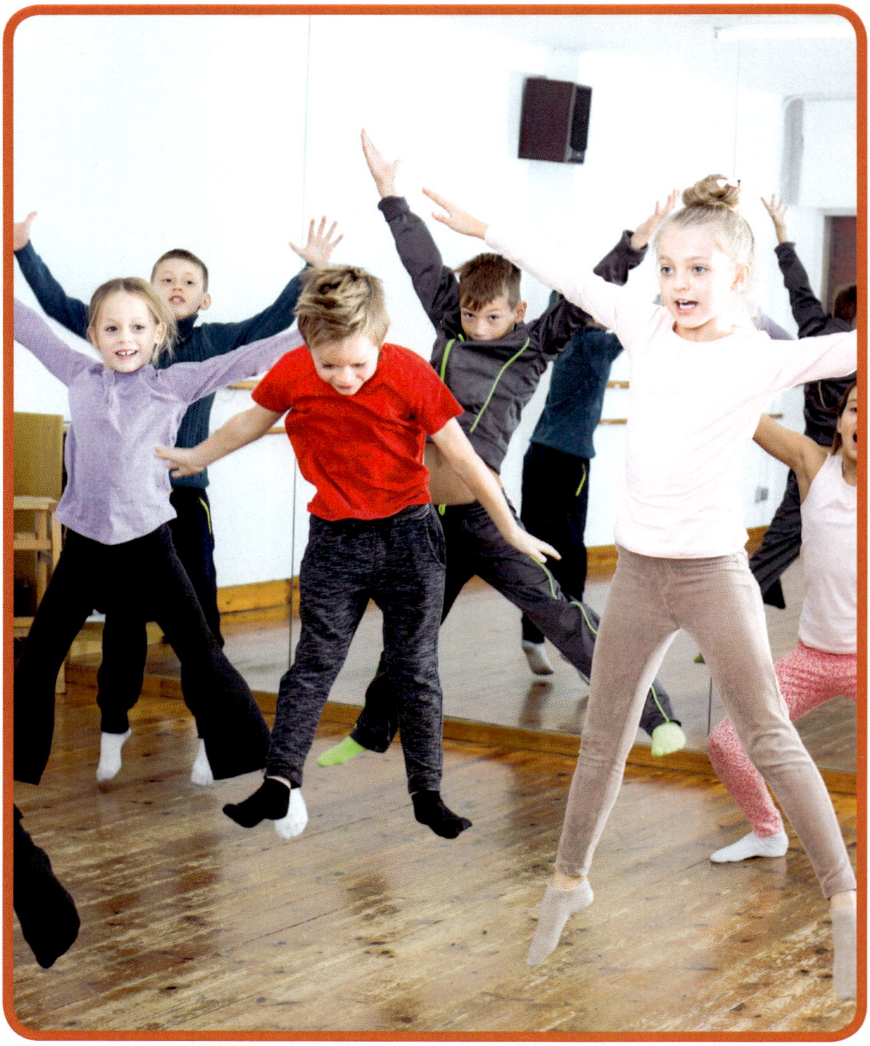

I can jump.

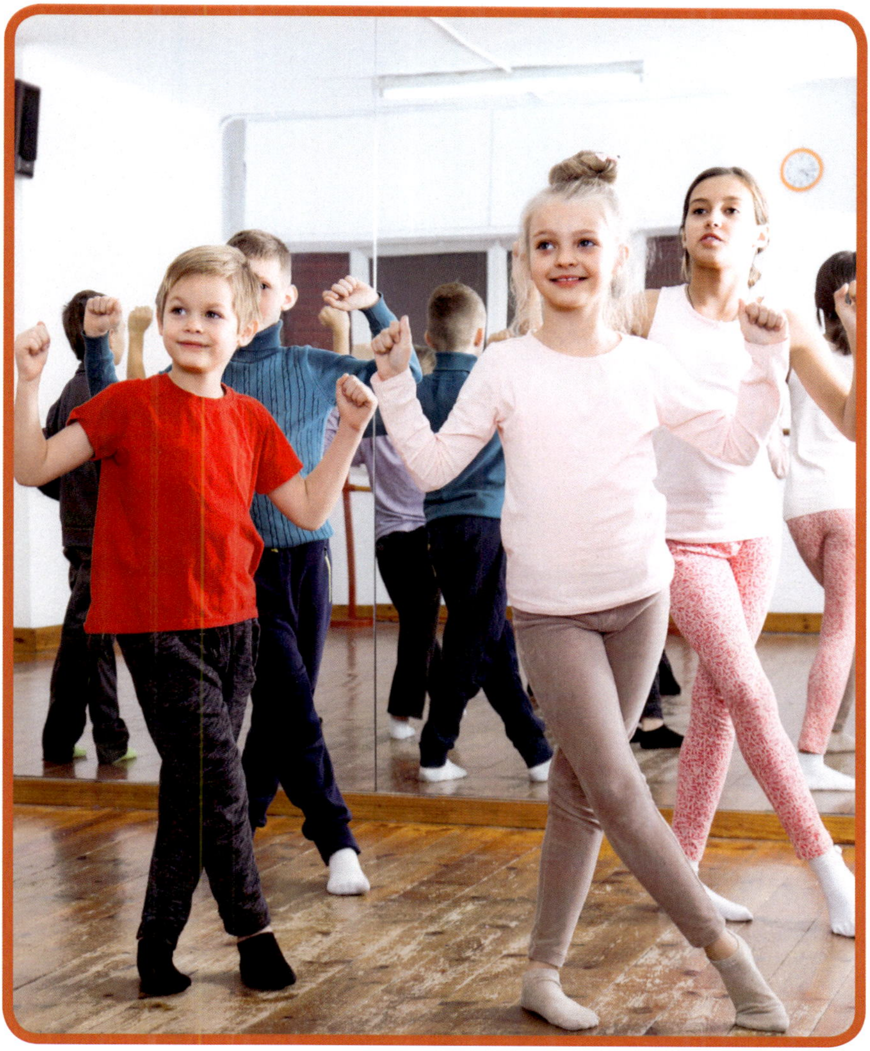

I can spin.

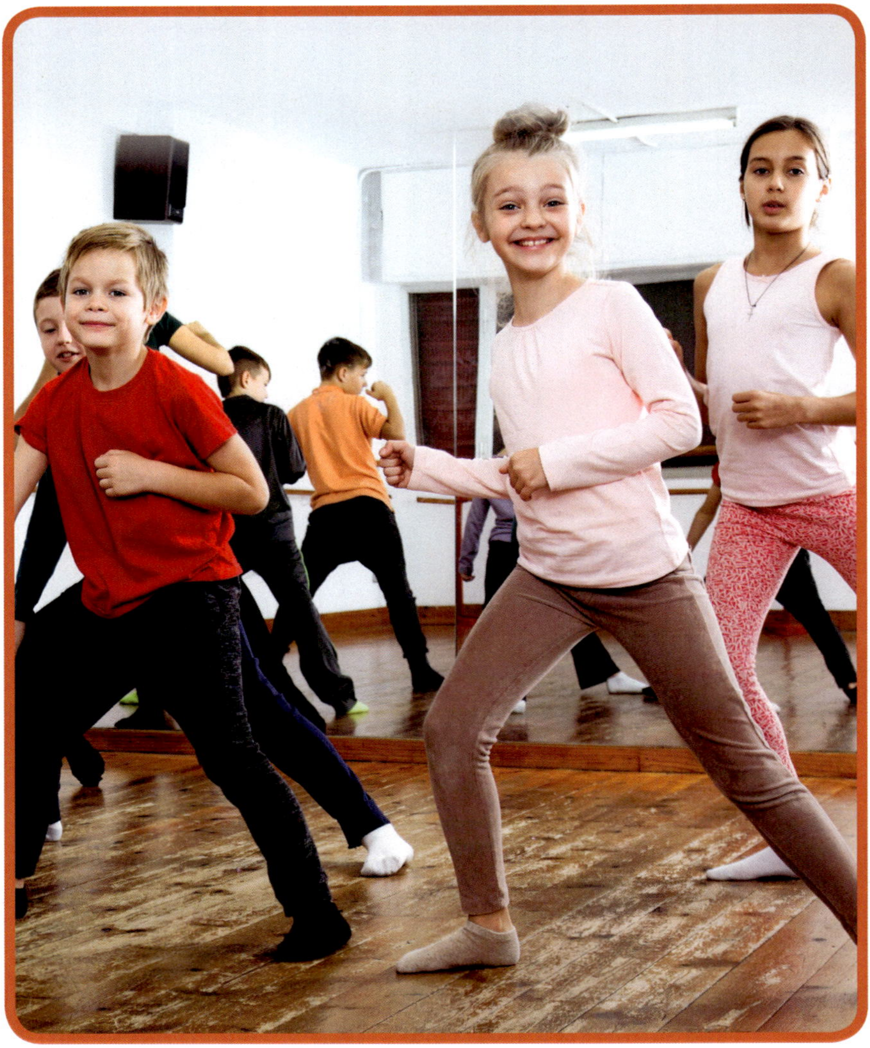

I can dance.

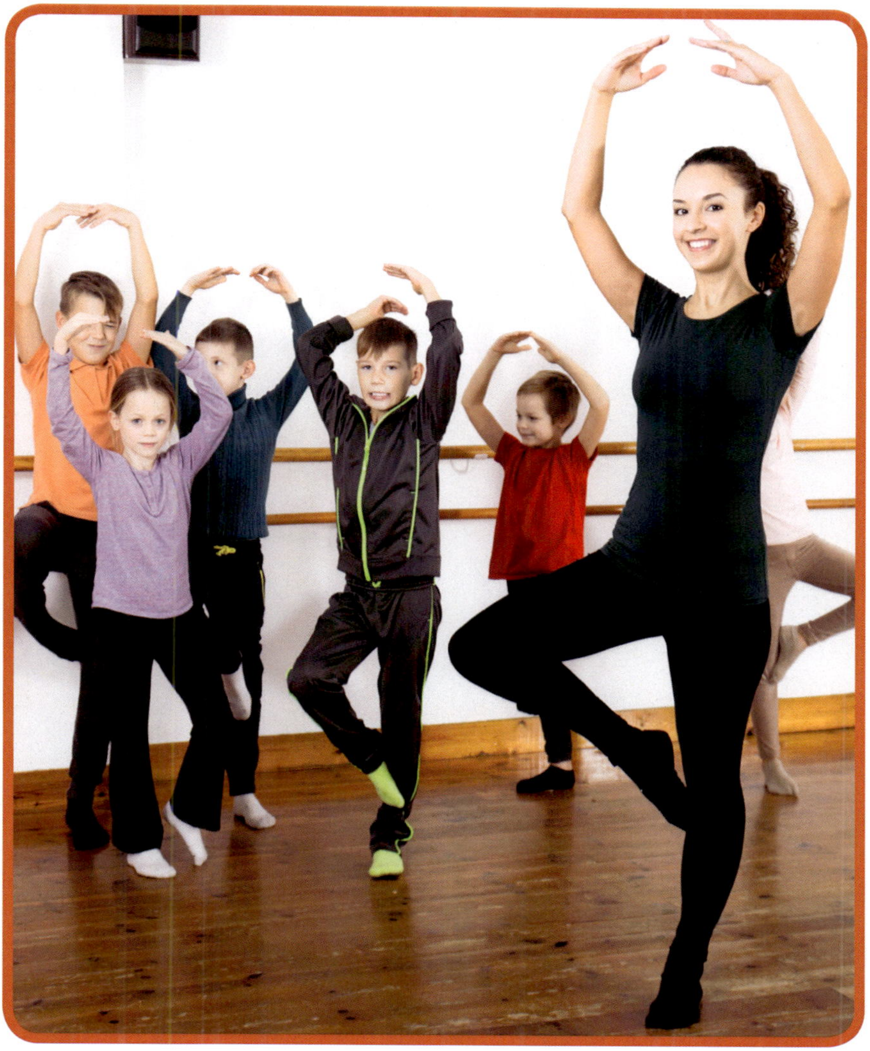

I can do my best.

Words to Know

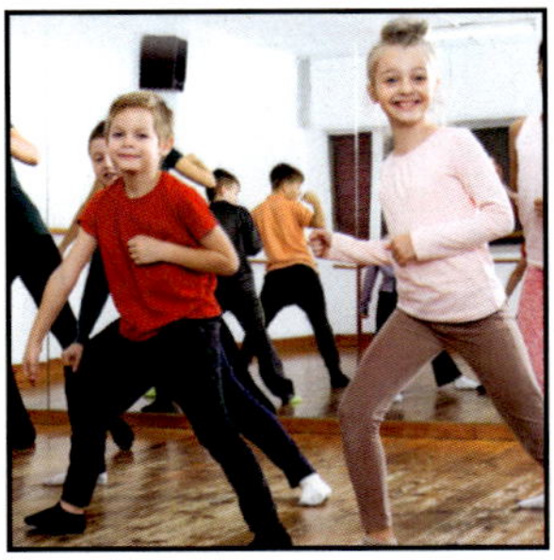

dance

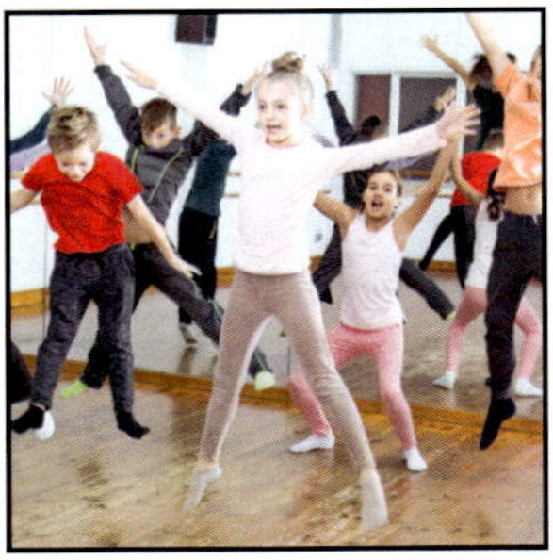

jump

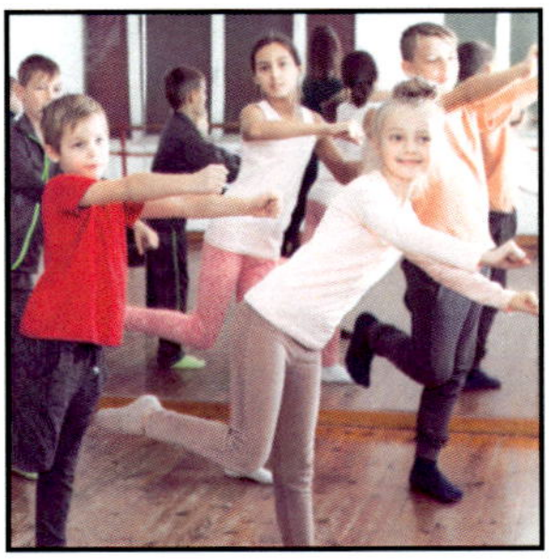

kick